Cipe Pineles
Two Remembrances

BY ESTELLE ELLIS

AND CAROL BURTIN FRIPP

CIPE

PINELES

**Cipe Pineles
Two Remembrances**

BY ESTELLE ELLIS
AND CAROL BURTIN FRIPP

GRAPHIC DESIGN ARCHIVES
CHAPBOOK SERIES: TWO

RIT
CARY GRAPHIC ARTS PRESS
2005

Cipe Pineles:
Two Remembrances
by Estelle Ellis
and Carol Burtin Fripp

RIT Cary Graphic Arts Press
90 Lomb Memorial Drive
Rochester, New York 14623-5604
http://wally.rit.edu/cary/carypress.html

Unless otherwise credited, all illustrations are used with permission of the
Cipe Pineles Collection, Archives and Special Collections, RIT Libraries,
Rochester Institute of Technology, with thanks and appreciation to Carol
Burtin Fripp and Thomas Golden. Every reasonable effort has been made
to contact copyright holders of materials reproduced in this book.
Corrections should be addressed to RIT Cary Graphic Arts Press.

Front cover: Feingersh. *Cipe Pineles*, ca. 1955. Gelatin silver print, 8 x 10 in.
Back cover: E.I. Jacoby. *Cipe Pineles at* Charm, ca. 1956. Gelatin silver
    print contact sheet, detail, 2¼ in. square.
Opposite: Cipe Pineles. *Drawn stamp on birthday card for Will Fripp*,
n.d. Felt marker, 4 x 4½ in. folded. *Courtesy of Carol Burtin Fripp.*

ISBN 0-9759651-5-8, Printed in U.S.A.

Library of Congress Cataloging-in-Publication Data
Ellis, Estelle.
   Cipe Pineles : two remembrances / by Estelle Ellis and Carol Burtin Fripp.
      p. cm. -- (Graphic design archives chapbook series ; 2)
   ISBN 0-9759651-5-8
   1. Golden, Cipe Pineles. 2. Graphic arts--United States--Biography. I.
Golden, Cipe Pineles. II. Burtin Fripp, Carol. III. Title. IV. Series.
   NC975.5.G59E43 2005
   741.6'092--DC22
                 2004028074

Cipe Pineles

Mr. Webster defines fashion as a way
of conforming. It might offend the painters
to be labeled conformists. It might even
offend the graphic designers. But that isn't by
intention here. I think any visual manifestation
can and should serve as inspiration to a
designer. But I think we ought to feed on
abstraction with great care. It can be pretty
indigestible. Graphic design can be useless
if it communicates nothing.

From an unpublished manuscript, *The Chemise in Typography*.

FOREWORD

Kari Horowicz
Art and Photography Librarian
RIT Libraries

THE GRAPHIC DESIGN ARCHIVES CHAPBOOK SERIES CELEBRATES achievements of the key graphic design pioneers whose work is documented in the Graphic Design Archive of the Archives and Special Collections, RIT Libraries, Rochester Institute of Technology.

The evolution of the series continues with this second volume on the life of Cipe Pineles, (1908–1991), one of the most prominent designers of the twentieth century and one of the first female art directors of a major magazine. The Cipe Pineles collection came to the RIT Special Collections 1991 and was deposited by Cipe Pineles's two adopted children: Tom Golden and Carol Burtin Fripp.

The Pineles collection includes images in all media–elegant pen-and-ink letters and notes, beautiful illustrations in gouache, (one of Cipe's favored media), and striking layout designs with dynamic sketches in miniature created with economy of line and color. In addition, there are innumerable sketches, including logo designs, showing her thorough design process.

Cipe Pineles's significance in graphic design history began to develop shortly after her tenure at the Condé Nast publications of *Vogue, Vanity Fair,* and *House and Garden* where she worked under the tutelage of the art director Mehemed Fehmy Agha. Moving to *Glamour* (1939–1946), *Seventeen* (1947–1950), *Charm* (1950–1959), and *Mademoiselle* (1959–1960),

Pineles was the first woman art director of long standing. She played a key role during a time of great change and growth in the early twentieth century. One of her signature contributions was extending the visual nomenclature of editorial content by commissioning well-known fine artists and illustrators to illuminate text. For two decades she art-directed new and emerging mass-market publications targeted at women, in particular young and working women. After her career in the editorial world, she continued her work in the design field, working as design director at Lincoln Center and as a design instructor at Parsons School of Design. In addition, she achieved a number of distinctions in the graphic design arena including her election as the first woman member of the Art Director's Club. In 1975, she was inducted into the Art Director's Hall of Fame and received posthumously the American Institute of Graphic Arts (AIGA) Medal of Distinction in 1996. The most authoratative work to date on Cipe Pineles is Martha Scotford's *Cipe Pineles: A Life in Design*, published by w.w. Norton in 1999.

Cipe Pineles's impact on design history has been acknowledged in two important museum exhibitions documenting the history of design in America. The first, *Graphic Design in America: A Visual Language History*, was shown in 1989, and featured an accompanying exhibition catalog published by the Walker Art Center, Minneapolis, which incorporates an interview with Cipe Pineles, along with examples of her work. Recently, the Bard Graduate Center for Studies in the Decorative Arts, Design and Culture, New York, held an exhibition entitled *Women Designers in the U.S.A., 1900–2000: Diversity and Difference*, with an extensive catalog featuring seminal women designers including the work of Cipe Pineles.

Cipe Pineles, 1945
Joffe. Gelatin silver print, 10 × 8 in.

This book follows in the tradition of the style of chapbooks– a small informative booklet, with a strong visual emphasis, of popular tales, ballads, or tracts. In this chapbook we have called upon two women who knew her very well–Estelle Ellis, who worked with her very closely at *Seventeen* and *Charm*, and Carol Burtin Fripp, her adopted daughter–to write short reflections on the woman they knew and cherished. The result is two intimate views of a dynamic, charming, delightful, energetic, and warm person.

I would like to thank Estelle Ellis and Carol Burtin Fripp for their wonderful essays, as well as Tom Golden for sharing marvelous images drawn by Cipe, found in family mementos. I am grateful to Martha Scotford for allowing us to reproduce an abridged, timeline from her book, outlining the key moments in Cipe Pineles's life. An ongoing thanks to R. Roger Remington– the enthusiastic supporter of the growing Graphic Design Archives. I would also like to thank Professor Bruce Ian Meader for his expert design. A special thanks to David Pankow, Director of the Cary Graphic Arts Press for his continuing encouragement and also to Amelia Hugill-Fontanel and Marnie Soom for their expertise in print production.

"Chodachrome *[sp]* night…I am a regular *Vogue* cover," 1940
Cipe filled this spoof best-seller with comical illustrations and inside jokes that she shared with her husband, Bill Golden. Cipe Pineles, *My Life with the Crown Prince: An Exposé that Names Names*, 1940. Gouache, 10 × 18 in. *Courtesy of Tom Golden.*

Stretch, 1969

Clockwise from top:

Detail of layout schema for *Stretch*.

Ballpoint pen, 9⅝ × 9½ in.

Right and bottom right:

Ann Smith, *Stretch*. New York:

Cornerstone Library Publications,

1969. Cipe Pineles, designer,

Jeanne Lessner, photographer.

Cover, pages 24–25.

Bottom left: *Stretch* page mock-ups.

Pen-and-ink, 8 × 5 in. each.

Cipe Pineles
A Great Heart

BY CAROL BURTIN FRIPP

Cipe Pineles, 1965
Jane Rady Lynes. *Cipe at the wedding of Carol Burtin and Robert Fripp.* Gelatin silver print, 5⅞ × 7⅞ in. *Collection of Carol Burtin Fripp. Courtesy of Jane Rady Photography.*

CIPE PINELES BECAME MY MOTHER TWICE. ON JANUARY 26, 1961, my father and Cipe were married in her wonderful Stony Point house, surrounded by friends and Cipe's family. Cipe legally adopted me on June 29, 1973, and I became not just her step-daughter, but her daughter.

Cipe and Bill Golden had always been close family friends. Bill's sudden death, followed by my mother Hilde's death a year later, had left the survivors emotionally shell-shocked. When my father told me he would like to propose to Cipe, I embraced the idea. It was a way of becoming a family again, of having a center. I gained not only a new mother and a brother, but also uncles, aunts, and cousins from Cipe's family. This was a new and pleasurable experience for me, since my own blood relatives lived thousands of miles away from New York in Germany or South America.

I was eighteen years old when our family moved into the Filors Lane house, and I soon realized that my stepmother Cipe was much more than the Cipe I had known since childhood. I had always admired her style, her sense of humor, and Cipe as a role model. What I came to know was a woman of warmth, generosity, and affection, a great source of comfort and guidance.

Dear Carol
How nice for me that you
found more BOOK OF HOURS
postcards. Printed in England
I see. Should you come across
a complete set of 12 cards,
please buy them for me (at my
expense) otherwise I'll have
to go to England
Love Cipe

Handwritten note
Pen, folded card, 5¾ in. square.
Courtesy of Carol Burtin Fripp.

Cipe encouraged me to go outside myself and to expand my experiences. I worked in Turin, Italy for a summer at an international exhibition and studied in England for my junior year of university. We wrote to each other every few days, describing what was going in our lives and sending interesting or humorous newspaper clippings to each other. As a student at Barnard College, I spent most weekends, all holidays, and many weeknights in Stony Point. The Filors Lane house was home. It also represented Cipe, since so much of the look and feel of the house reflected her tastes and values.

I remember many dinner times, at the beautifully set dining room table or in the comfortable kitchen, with great food and challenging discussions. It was not mere dinnertime smalltalk! Politics and the world of design were the major topics. Often we had guests as well, especially on weekends, and I came to know many of Cipe's circle of friends. The house was filled with affection and activity.

Cipe set high standards for herself and others. Professionally, she had just ended her career as magazine art director when she married my father, but she continued to actively work on design projects, to be involved in the art world, and to create beauty around her. Every object in the Stony Point house looked good, from furnishings to wallpaper, to table and bed linens, to the soaps in the soap dishes, to the most modest hardware items. For years we had only a tiny Sony television set because it was the only attractive model sold. Both she and my father refused to encourage bad design. How happy they both were when a range of good-looking Braun appliances became available!

Will Burtin and Cipe Pineles, 1965
Jane Rady Lynes. *At Filors Lane, Stony Point, New York, during the wedding of Carol Burtin and Robert Fripp.* Gelatin silver print, 7⅞ × 5⅞ in. Collection of Carol Burtin Fripp. *Courtesy of Jane Rady Photography.*

In October 1965, Robert Fripp and I were married at the Filors Lane house. It was a warm, sunny day, and the ceremony and reception took place outside, with family and friends gathered on the patio. All of it was organized by Cipe since, until six weeks earlier, I had been working in England while Robert finished his university degree there. A month later, with my parents' support, Robert and I moved to Canada. We had been advised that Robert, as a green card carrying non-U.S. citizen, would have been quickly drafted into the U.S. army for the escalating Vietnam War. We thought the move would give us time to think and to plan what to do with our lives.

Over the next few years, we spent many vacations back in Stony Point, while Cipe and my father visited us frequently in Toronto. Our sons Eric, (born 1967), and Will, (born 1969), remember the long drives down to Rockland County and the enthusiastic welcome we always received when our 1965 Land Rover finally pulled into the driveway after eleven or twelve hours of sibling arguments, interspersed with stops for refreshments. The door of the house would be thrown open and Cipe would emerge, shouting "Hurray!" (and, sometimes, "Prosciutto!") Inside would be a big "Welcome Home" sign drawn by Cipe, and another by my father, and sometimes one by my brother, Tom. Simon, the grey cat, would come to check the boys out, and there was always the house to re-explore. Not to mention the big dish of prosciutto and melon sitting on the kitchen table.

As long as she lived, Cipe told me that she thought that the key function of her maternal role was to keep her daughter warm, which she interpreted as keeping me supplied with winter coats and wine. The winter coats came from her designer friends like Bonnie Cashin. Cipe later introduced me to Marimekko dresses and Coach handbags.

If we were visiting her, she would produce a case of wine for us to pack and take home with us. If she was visiting us, we would make a pilgrimage to the Ontario Liquor Licensing outlet since Cipe loved these government-run liquor stores. It was such a change from the more relaxed liquor laws in the U.S. where Cipe would invest heavily and enthusiastically on our behalf. She enjoyed going to our nearby supermarket, which she found rather exotic. Canadian labeling needed to be in both official languages of English and French and she enjoyed comparing the product designs.

I still remember the first time my parents visited us after we had bought our house in 1969. Much of the living room furniture; Eames chair, Saarinen chair and sofa–had come from my pre-Cipe parental home, taken out of storage, reupholstered, and shipped north. It was a semi-familiar setting that they found themselves visiting. At the supermarket, my father discovered (and bought in quantity) a kind of dark German pumpernickle he remembered from his youth in Cologne. Cipe fell in love with the leopard-fur-pattern cover design of a Canadian brand of Kleenex tissues, and bought a whole carton. When we took them to the airport for their flight back to New York, my father packed his breads into his suitcase, and Cipe had filled an entire case with the tissue boxes. At the customs inspection, Cipe's case was opened first. The inspector looked suspiciously at the tissue boxes, and then at Cipe. "You see," she began, "I am an artist." He hastily shut her suitcase, and opened my father's, where he discovered all of the breads. "Don't tell me," he muttered, and moved rapidly away from these obviously-crazy people.

A Good Night's Rest

The botanical illustrations in this image are from Cipe's personal collection. Mimi Sheraton, "A Good Night's Rest." *Seventeen*, February 1950, 106–107. Cipe Pinleles, art director, Dan Wynn, photographer. *Courtesy of Hearst Communications.*

Bernarda Shahn and Cipe Pineles, 1975

Cipe in Rhodes with friend, Bernarda Shahn, wife of illustrator Ben Shahn. Gelatin silver print, 7 × 5 in.
Courtesy of Carol Burtin Fripp.

In January 1972, my father died after several months struggle with mesothelioma, an asbestos-related cancer possibly acquired previously from the asbestos used in pre-plastics days for modeling designs. This was a devastating period for Cipe and for me. My children and I were in New York for the final few weeks of my father's life, and Robert joined us when work permitted. Cipe and I had always been close, but now we became even closer. About two months later, Cipe asked if I would "mind it" if she adopted me. According to the law, she had ceased to be my stepmother upon my father's death. Mind it! I told her I would be honored, and that—law or not— I thought of her as my mother.

And so, in June of 1972, I found myself being interviewed by a New York State Welfare official in Spring Valley, New York, sitting on a tiny chair meant for a three-year old. They didn't expect adoptees to be twenty-nine years old. Part of the official process was to ensure that I, as the adoptive child, was not being taken advantage of by my former stepmother. A year later, the adoption was finalized, and we became "legal" again.

What do I remember when I think of Cipe? I remember her discovering the interests of each of my sons, and encouraging them. I remember her taking Eric to museums, and teaching Will calligraphy. I remember the family outings to Shakespeare and Gilbert & Sullivan in Central Park. I remember Stony Point family dinners, and the dinner parties crowded with friends and great conversation. I remember how the only acceptable flavor of ice cream in Cipe's house was vanilla. (My father used to sneak out to a nearby Carvel occasionally for a sundae, warning me, "Don't tell Cipe!") I remember Cipe giving me an annual gold safety pin from Tiffany, to create a collection like her own.

Eric Fripp, 1973
Encouraged by Cipe, Eric Fripp, age 6, uses his blocks to create type. Gelatin silver print, 3½ × 5 in. *Courtesy of Carol Burtin Fripp.*

I remember Cipe's anger at injustice. I remember the pleasure Cipe found in her vegetable garden. I remember her Schiaparelli pink notepads. I remember Cipe's weekly grocery shopping forays with Utah Mascoll, her Trinidadian helper (and later, friend), and Cipe trying to teach Utah to drive.

I remember Cipe's visits to Toronto, and her pleasure at discovering a delicious dish called "Rainbow in Crystal Fold" at our favorite Chinese restaurant, a dish that–try as she might– she could never find in New York. I remember her phoning me, when both children were very small, to say that she and my father had decided that Eric and Will should have some good maple blocks. We then discovered as a moving van pulled up in front of the house that "some" blocks appeared to be the entire wooden blocks department from Creative Playthings! Another year, after Buckminster Fuller had spoken at one of my father's conferences, a geodesic dome "for the boys to climb on" in our back yard was delivered by another moving van.

I remember the hand-drawn birthday cards, each one a work of art, which arrived for all of our birthdays, and the many telephone conversations we had. I remember going to Cipe for advice, and her coming to Robert and me for advice, especially in her later years. And most of all, I remember her affection, and her great heart.

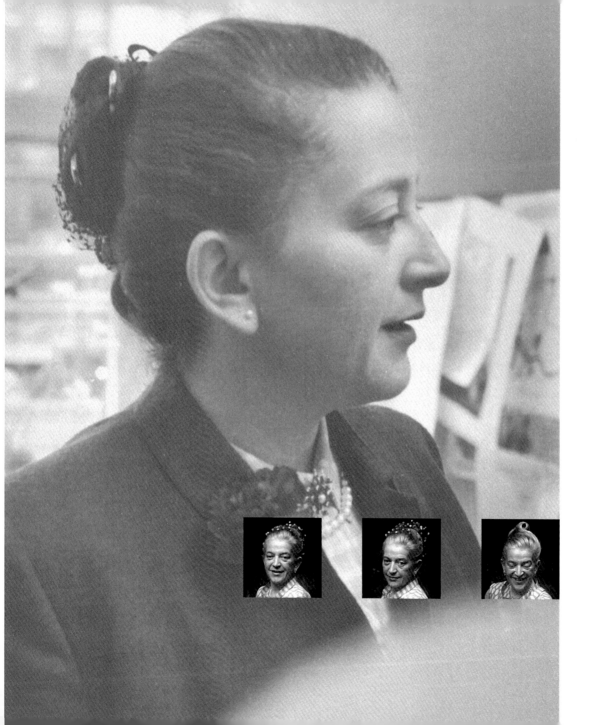

Cipe Pineles
Pioneer in An Historic Time of Change

BY ESTELLE ELLIS

CIPE...C.P...CIPE PINELES (PIN-ELES) HER NAME. HER SIGNATURE, C.P., was as singular as she was, as unique as the body of work that is her legacy and as rare as the relationships she fostered. Cipe was an original. She was like no other—like the one-of-a-kind discoveries she taught us to appreciate.

When I met Cipe, she was thirty-nine and I was twenty-eight. The woman who brought us together, Helen Valentine, who invented *Seventeen* magazine, was fifty-four. We vaulted a generation chasm without being conscious of it. In the words of Cipe's husband, William Golden (creator of the iconic CBS eye) we became an unstoppable, synergistic troika as editor, art director, and promotion director.

We worked together for thirteen halcyon years, creating two magazines that made publishing history: *Seventeen* from 1947 to 1950, and *Charm* (later merged with *Glamour*) from 1950 to 1959. They alerted the nation to the social and economic importance of two heretofore invisible segments of the population—teenagers and working women. Their meteoric circulation and advertising growth signaled the changing world of women, the rising independence and dominance of youth and their combined, unprecedented spheres of influence and buying power. The galaxy of products and services invented for them generated a new era of editorial, industrial, and graphic design. This was a world in which Cipe worked and excelled in and introduced me to share with her.

Left: Feingersh. *Cipe Pineles*, ca. 1955. Gelatin silver print, 8 x 10 in.
3 left, above: Jerry Cooke. *Cipe Pineles*, 1966. Gelatin silver prints, 2 x 1⅜ in. each. *Courtesy of the photographer.*

We became devoted colleagues and life-long friends. The work and home lives we shared illuminated the breakthrough, supportive roles of women in the second half of the 20th century.

Looking back, we were pioneers in an historic time of social, economic, and cultural change. World War II would profoundly alter our lives, giving women the opportunity to participate in the transformation of the multi-faceted world of women's magazines and the design industry. The respect Helen and Cipe had for each other, their colleagues, and the master artists, photographers, typographers, and production people they trusted, taught me the art and skills of collaboration. To witness their creative interaction and participate in their vigorous interchange of ideas and opinions was empowering. I inherited Helen's love of words and Cipe's eye for art and design. They helped me understand how creative people can energize each other and they showed me how to integrate and benefit from what was clearly their counterpoint cultural backgrounds, mores, and work styles.

Helen Valentine, Cipe Pineles, and Estelle Ellis, ca. 1968
Gelatin silver print, 4 × 2 in.
Courtesy of Estelle Ellis.

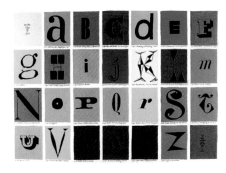

Birthday Card for Tom Golden, 1970
Complete alphabet and detail.
Gouache, 18 × 23¾ in.

Helen Valentine was an only child and a first generation American who was raised by German immigrant parents in a protective, controlling environment. She was shaped by their authoritarian values and would emphasize the importance of an orderly, "appropriate" approach to writing, editing, design, business behavior, and relationships. "Never use a contraction when writing to academics," she censored in the margin of a letter I had written to the president of a university. In sharp contrast, Cipe came to the United States, with a closely bonded family of protective brothers and sisters, from war-devastated, dictator-repressed Poland and Austria. Their joyful discovery of liberty and opportunity in an adventurous America generated Cipe's drive to achieve and her aversion to conformity. This was the explanation she gave for her free-style approach to design and art direction. "Don't worry about a mistake you've made," she would counsel me. "Learn from it, embrace it, use it! It can lead you in a new direction. It can help you discover the untried, the unusual, something more wonderful." She demonstrated this one day. When a headline didn't fit, instead of reworking it, she let it flow along the outer margin, perpendicular to the text block. The effect was startling and modern.

Charm, January 1954
Cipe Pineles, art director, William Helburn, photographer. 11¼ × 8½ in.

Cipe taught me the critical importance of the partnership between writer and designer, editor and art director, art director and printer. Nothing was more instructive than going with her to a printer, standing with her in a pressroom and listening to her talk to the men who were working on her project. She would insist on knowing their names and would cajole them, ever so gently, to go back again and again to get the colors right.

"Let the foreman in the printing plant know you're going to baby-sit the job," she would emphasize. "They do a better job when they know that you respect your craft. Don't wait for them to send the proofs to you. Care enough to see something you've designed through to the finish." Unforgettable are the times Cipe would retrieve a bundle of make-ready press sheets, layered with a jumble of color and type, bringing them back to her office where she would hang them on the wall like works of art. Repeatedly she would remind us that misprints are treasures; they remind us that people, not machines, made them.

Cipe opened our eyes to a world of disparate and wonderful things: shocking pink envelopes, pharmaceutical glass and pottery, Floris soap, English watering cans, rose-garlanded porcelain cats, leather-bound diaries, white knob dressmaker pins, Limoges china, Will's mercury glass, calligraphy books and pens, type sheets and type trays, Conklin's orchard apples and Fire Island beach plum jelly, French chef copper-bottomed cookware and precision-tooled cheese knives from Germany, brisket and kasha, champagne flutes, and peasant bread.

Travel journal, 1970

Cipe decorated this journal for Estelle and her family on the occasion of their trip to Paris. Ballpoint pen, 8½ × 5½ in. *Courtesy of Estelle Ellis.*

Cipe made the ordinary become extraordinary and the extraordinary became accessible. Her inimitable handwriting and artwork made her letters, notes, envelopes, personalized gift-wraps, and labels become Cipe-collectibles. No one who received them could bear to throw them away. They became treasured keepsakes and we mounted them for a private one-woman show on her sixty-fifth birthday. Most memorable to me were the artist's sketchbooks that Cipe transformed into travel journals for her friends and family and the joyful monograms (name paintings) she created to celebrate birthdays and anniversaries.

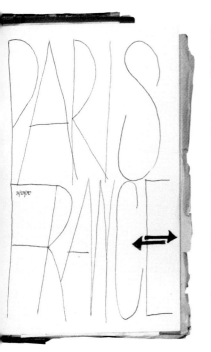

Cipe at *Charm*, ca. 1956
E.I. Jacoby. *Cipe in the offices of* Charm
magazine. Gelatin silver print contact
sheet, detail, 2¼ in. square.

Cipe, 1971
Self-portrait caricature for the
Parsons School of Design yearbook.
Pen-and-ink, 8 × 5⅛ in.

Cipe set her own style in everything she did—the way she lived, the way she worked, and the way she dressed. She discarded the drawing board for a glass-topped table that framed eighteenth century botanical prints. She entertained a diverse blend of friends in her *gemütlich* kitchen, cooking dinner while they watched, then went about arranging a large, round oak table in the adjacent dining room with mismatched plates and napkins. The contrarian way Cipe dressed defined her. Her old world, *démodé* wardrobe created an indelible image. She was an anachronism in the up-tempo, revolving world of fashion in which she worked. Cipe dressed down, ignoring the dictates and fluidity of style changes and trends. She projected an image of earthy simplicity, preferring loose-fitting Marimekko print dresses, billowy skirts, and vintage blouses anchored by the signature piece of jewelry she created—a dangling clutch of graduated, gold safety pins from Tiffany. Her hair was swept up in a topknot wrapped in a diaphanous fabric.

Cipe was equally memorable in the way she talked. She had a mellifluous Viennese accent that she never lost, her critical view of business and politics, her self-mocking honesty, and ironic sense of humor. Her magnetic presence and influence was as strong as her graphic imprint. Her ocean-crossing, generation-spanning friends became her extended family and remained close to her throughout her life. Wherever artists, designers, illustrators, men, and women in the graphic crafts gathered to honor, inform, or support each other Cipe was there. From Aspen's design conference in Colorado to AIGA meetings in Amsterdam, Greece, Poland, and Venice. In turn, her friends were there for her.

They cheered for her when she broke the sex barrier and became the first woman invited to join the men's only New York Art Directors Club in 1943–a distinction she held for forty-seven years. They gave her a standing ovation at the United Nations in 1975 when she was inducted into the Art Industry Director's Hall of Fame. Cipe became its nineteenth "Unsung Pioneer," joining a pantheon of design greats that notably included her renowned, deceased husbands, Bill Golden and Will Burtin.

New York Art Directors Club, 1948
Cipe Pineles's membership certificate.
Print, 11¼ × 8¾ in.

Seventeen's Calendar for 1949
Cipe Pineles, "Summer," *Seventeen*,
December 1948, 70–71.
Gouache, 10½ × 6¾ in.
Courtesy of Hearst Communications.

What can be said about Cipe that her life's work doesn't demonstrate? She was fearless, intuitive, and inventive. In addition to participating in the art direction of American and British *Vogue* in her very young years, she designed four trailblazing twentieth-century women's magazines: *Seventeen*, *Charm, Glamour,* and *Mademoiselle*. In the six decades that span her career, she stunned the publishing world by becoming not only the first art director for women's magazines, but the art director for the first magazine for teenagers and working women. Cipe read her readers well, anticipating their yearning and drive for independence. She respected and was responsive to the intelligence and openness of young people. She identified with and supported time-pressed women who, like herself, were coping with the multi-task responsibilities of job and home. She illuminated their need for inspiration and information. Cipe introduced a new generation of daughters and their mothers to a sophisticated magazine aesthetic that embraced fine art, photography, contemporary product, and publication design. Her biographer, Martha Scotford, Professor of Graphic Design at North Carolina State University, quoted Cipe as saying that she was determined "to broaden the visual experience of her readers."

Following these fifteen precedent-setting years in magazine publishing, Cipe embarked on a second career. She "hung up her own shingle," joining Will Burtin in his internationally known design studio. It was here that she was commissioned to develop identity programs for the Lincoln Center and the Parsons School of Design, both of which won awards for their innovative concepts and riveting designs.

**Seventeen,
May 1948**
Cipe Pineles,
art director,
Francesco Scavullo,
photographer.
13 × 10½ in.
*Courtesy of Hearst
Communications.*

Parsons Bread Book, 1974
Comprehensive cover layout designed
by Parsons students in Cipe's editorial
design class. Gelatin silver print, pencil,
gouache. 11 × 8½ in.
Courtesy, Parsons School of Design,
New School University, New York,
New York.

Parsons celebrated Cipe's twentieth anniversary by establishing a
communications design scholarship in her name. Frank Stanton,
President of CBS, introduced her to a standing room audience
with this succinct accolade: "Cipe, the consummate designer
and educator." A dazzling exhibition of the communications
publication program she conceived and directed for Parsons for
the past twenty-five years, framed the room. Posters, yearbooks,
study catalogs and ads for New York and California schools,
demonstrated her ingenuity, uncompromising standards, and
influence. Cipe frequently engaged her students in these projects
in order to expose them to the benefits of creative partnership
and to help them vault the chasm between classroom and
workplace. She encouraged her students to think differently
and to break away from conventional concepts and practices.
An example of this was when she involved them in the
making of Parsons iconoclastic, award-winning yearbooks that
recorded the lives, times, and talent of her young students.
The audacious cover of one of these spelled out the word
"Bread" in ten different typefaces. Traditional portraits and
profiles of graduating seniors and classroom scenes were
displaced by student-photographed and student-crafted "staff
of life" sculptures. This included a scenic tour of New York's
multi-ethnic heritage bakeries and master bakers. The foreword
of the yearbook credits its graduates with "sifting, rolling, and
shaping" the content—a six month classroom project conceived
and directed by a teacher who reminded her students to associate
the word "bread" with craft and not the vernacular word for
money. Cipe's signature, unsigned drawings complement the
contents page and inside cover.

Think of everything that's happened since they were born and you'll begin to understand the new college generation

Since we were born
Jackie Meyer
Lettering

The Drug Culture	STEREO
WORKING MOTHERS	POPE JOHN
Women's Lib	CARNABY STREET
BLACK POWER	DRUG ABUSE
LYNDON B. JOHNSON	THE COMPUTER
Synthetics	KENT STATE
MARIJUANA	TELEVISION
Vietnam	RICHARD M. NIXON
zero population	Chicago '68
BERKLEY	The Pill
THE BEATLES	Watergate
Legal Abortion	Polio Vaccine
AUTOMATION	WOODSTOCK
CEASAR CHAVEZ	John F. Kennedy
RALPH NADER	WATTS
School Desegregation	CIVIL RIGHTS BILL
HIPPIES, YIPPIES	jet travel
SANITARIUM	NUCLEAR TESTING
Martin Luther King	man on the moon
TRANSISTORS	The 18 Year Old Vote
Amnesty	INFLATION

Since We Were Born, 1974

Since We Were Born, New York:
Parsons School of Design, 1974. 8½ × 11 in.
Top: Pages 3–4. Above: Cover.
*Courtesy, Parsons School of Design,
New School University, New York, New York.*

In 1974, Cipe drew her senior design students' attention to a full-page ad that my company, Business Image, Inc., had created for one of its Condé Nast clients, *Glamour* magazine. To understand the new college generation it urged, "Think of everything that happened since they were born." A word list was developed of the awesome events, discoveries and people that impacted young men and women for two decades.

It inspired Cipe's graduating class and ignited the powerful thoughts, images, and feelings they unleashed in Parsons's 1974 yearbook. Cipe was persuaded that this time, photographs of graduating seniors were essential to a yearbook design. She arranged a dramatic checkerboard of two hundred expressive, young faces–candid student shot photos–for the front, back, and inside covers of a yearbook she titled "Since We Were Born." It documents their talent and response to one of the most tumultuous periods in American history.

Cipe understood, thoroughly enjoyed, and easily connected with young people throughout her career. She chose them to work with her on a diversity of challenging design projects. She taught them, mentored them, hired them, and recommended them for jobs with her many well-positioned friends throughout the world. She was a seminal force shaping the careers of several generations of aspiring men and women who went on to achieve successful careers in the publication, advertising, graphic arts, and design industries.

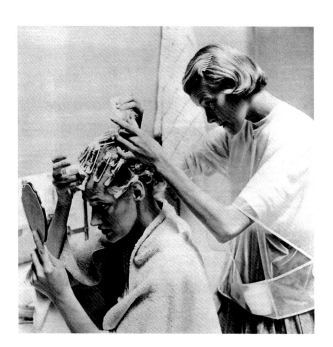

Big Apple Sunrise, 1981
Janet Amendola. Colored pencil and acrylic on paper, 4½ × 9½ in. Cipe Pineles, art director. *Courtesy of the artist.*

Beauty Begins at Home
Jean Campbell, "Beauty Begins at Home." *Seventeen*, October 1949, 102–103. Cipe Pinleles, art director, Lillian Bassman, photographer. *Courtesy of Hearst Communications.*

Sunday Afternoon
Lucile Vaughan Payne, "Sunday
Afternoon." *Seventeen*, September 1949,
126. Cipe Pinleles, art director,
Ben Shahn, illustrator.
Courtesy of Hearst Communications.

The Fur Coat
Anne Strick, "The Fur Coat." *Seventeen*,
December 1948, 83. Cipe Pinleles,
art director, Jacob Lawrence, illustrator.
Courtesy of Hearst Communications.

Although I left Cipe and Helen in 1958 to focus on my own
business, the bond that glued us together, personally and
professionally, remained strong and nurturing throughout our
lives. Helen was there for me when my first child was born.
She paced the hospital corridor with my husband. Cipe was there
for me when I furnished my first apartment and again when
I set out on my first solo career flight. Cipe called me every day
for three months when I was contemplating my "next step."
She would insist that I get out of the house, meet her for lunch,
walk with her through museums or join her at Edith Halpert's
Downtown Gallery where she introduced me to the work of
Kunyoshi, Jacob Lawrence, Raphael Soyer, Ben Shahn, and the
other artists she would persuade to enhance the fiction pages of
Seventeen. She kept up my spirits and confidence, reminding me
that an unanswered call was someone I wouldn't want to connect
with or work for, and that my name was enough, and that I didn't
have to say I was from a magazine to gain access or attention.
She insisted "no one less that Bill Golden" should design the
letterhead for my new business and both of them argued against
my calling it "Business Image." "Your name is your calling card,
your client will be buying you, not your company," she said.
We compromised by including both names in my letterhead.

Handwritten note, 1979
Courtesy of Estelle Ellis.

House on Filors Lane
Stony Point, New York.
Gelatin silver print, 5 × 7 in.

Our lifelong friendship embraced our families and was reinforced by the respect and support from our husbands and the admiration they had for our unique partnership. Miraculously, they enjoyed each other as well. They were rare men for their times—proud of and unthreatened by our achievements—partners in sharing the pressures dual working parents experience. Our children grew up together. Helen's two granddaughters, my son and daughter, and Cipe's son, Tom, frequented each other's homes. We celebrated birthdays, graduations, weddings, and holidays together in New York, on Fire Island, and in Stony Point when Cipe moved to her storybook house on Filors Lane. It was a magnet for the young and not so young—a resting, nesting, and renewal place for Rockland County neighbors, worldly New Yorkers, and international travelers. It was everything Cipe was—warm, welcoming, and bountiful in beauty.

The house was a serendipitous assemblage of objects, books, and art with books piled on tables and arranged invitingly in mirror-backed bookcases. The walls on every floor were covered with the heirloom quilts that Will brought to their marriage and the art came from friends, Ben and Bernarda Shahn, Lucille Corcos and Edgar Levy, Richard Lindner, Joe Kaufman, and young Tom, of course.

The Visual Craft of William Golden, 1962
Cipe Pineles and Kurt Weihs, designers. New York: George Braziller, Inc. 1962. *Courtesy of CBS Photo Archive.*

Pineles-Burtin wedding, 1961
Helen Valentine, Cipe Pineles, Estelle Ellis, and their husbands at Cipe's wedding to Will Burtin. Gelatin silver print. *Courtesy of Estelle Ellis.*

Much has been acknowledged about Cipe's pioneering role in the design profession. Her adventurous approach to designing magazines and her unconventional approach to teaching design is significant. She made a bold decision to commission the nation's most notable artists to create original art for a young fashion magazine and she possessed a unique talent for drawing, painting, and collaborating with writers, artists, and editors. But what was most intriguing was Cipe's personal magnetism. It resulted in the most synergistic of partnerships, first, through marriage to William Golden, and secondly, after he died in 1959, to Will Burtin. Both men were influential in the design industry.

Many have wondered how these two assertive, individualistic talents related to Cipe as well as their influence on her work and career. "Respectfully and productively" was my reply. Their lives were intertwined creatively. Although different temperamentally, they shared each other's design aesthetics and values, and they collaborated throughout their career lives. Cipe and Bill were married for 17 years. Their professional lives grew on an upward course that paralleled the advancement of the American graphic design industry. Cipe's union with Will Burtin expanded her knowledge and appreciation of the world of European design. Their counterpoint personalities complemented each other. Cipe was outgoing. Bill and Will were introverted but receptive to Cipe's gregarious, buoyant embrace of people and new experiences. She softened their protective armor. She was candid about the differences and similarities in the way they worked, the people they chose to work with and that they brought into her life—the writers and artists that Bill shared with her, the scientists and philosophers that Will introduced her to. Both men expanded Cipe's diverse world of people, resources, design concepts, and solutions. Both heightened her professional skills and techniques.

LINCOLN CENTER ANNUAL REPORT 1967-68

Cipe recollected, in a interview with Gertrude Snyder in the September 1978 issue of *Upper and Lowercase*, about being married to two celebrated designers:

> It wasn't always easy, and we had lots more things to quarrel about than do most couples, like: Why does that artist do a decent job for you and never one as good for me? Or: Should you ever use anything but sans serif type, and if yes, when? Or: How come they asked only you to be a judge at that show, relegating me to socialize with the wives at the pool?

> When Bill and I married, we had been working independently and had to some extent recognizable styles of our own. Each of us respected and admired the other's work. We liked to compare daily disasters, and often came up with better solutions to problems by letting off steam. I learned a lot from Bill: one was to accept a raise and return it to the company the next day in exchange for a four-day week. The other thing I learned was how to say "no" to intrusive demands.

Lincoln Center, 1968
Left: Cipe's ballpoint pen logo sketches. Bottom left: Pen-and-ink cover layout and the final solution for Lincoln Center's annual report. 11 × 8½ in. each.
Courtesy, Archives of Lincoln Center for the Performing Arts, Inc.

Child Welfare League of America, ca. 1966
Cipe's experimentation with photo-stats for CWLA's corporate identity. Various cut and pasted sheets.

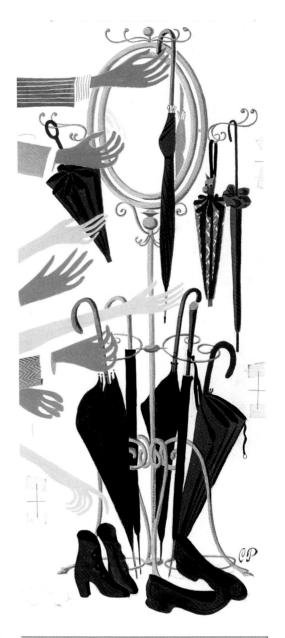

Illustrations by Cipe Pineles

Clockwise from top: Holiday card for Ruth and
Frank Stanton. Screen print, detail, 9½ × 7½ in.
Right and below right: Illustrations for Jack Stenbuck,
"When He Says 'Rain'…It Rains!" *Coronet* magazine,
January 1947. Gouache, 11 × 9 in. and detail, 14½ × 8 in.
Below left: Gouache, 12⅛ × 12⅛ in.

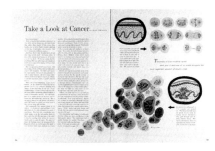

Cipe Pineles, art director

Top: Jean Campbell, "Take a Look at Cancer." *Seventeen,* April 1948, 102–103. Mary Lorenc, illustrator. Center: Eileen Murphy, "Take a New Look at Libraries." *Seventeen,* March 1948, 138–139. Joe Kaufman, illustrator. Bottom: Janet Bastian, "Want to be an Aquabelle?" *Seventeen,* July 1948, 46–47. Jerome Snyder, illustrator.

I look back on my time with Will Burtin with gratitude. Though Bill and Will share the same profession, two more dissimilar temperaments I can't imagine. Both had rigorous standards of design. Will, perhaps because he was trained in Cologne, was more rigid, less flexible in decision-making. Bill, equally diamond-sharp in his philosophy, had a more fluid approach to a design solution. After Will and I married, I gave up my job to join his office. Will's commissions required frequent trips here and abroad. He felt it urgent for designers to communicate with designers, writers, philosophers all over the world, and I was free to go with him. Will and I worked on separate projects. The scientific data that stimulated him to design 3-D structures was a little much for me.

On the other hand, he felt my attitude on type was frivolous. I was pretty good at type specifications, but sometimes Will would sit beside me and without a word, redo them. It made me furious then, but I do them now the Will Burtin way.

Bill and Will were masters in choosing type and although they worked with the best typographers in New York City, they would frequently "reconfigure" a headline to increase readability and engagement. Cipe learned the refinements of typesetting from them and adopted a similar hands-on approach to the process. She would meticulously cut the type apart to reduce or increase space between words, letters and lines to intensify visual impact. Her inimitable style of hand-lettering further distinguished her work. "Type is to read," she would quote Bill. "A well chosen typeface or font can transform words into art." And she would add: "It is the designer's right to rewrite a headline if it improves the page."

Twenty Color-Explosive Years, 1965

Right: *House and Garden* commissioned Estelle Ellis's company, Business Image, to produce this promotional brochure in celebration of its color-forecasting program. Cipe Pineles designed the color pattern so each combination of four squares would be color-compatible. This piece inspired the theme of this chapbook's cover.
Offset print, 11 × 17 in.
Courtesy of Estelle Ellis.

Cipe's signature
Sketchbook label.

The other writers, as well as me, didn't contest Cipe's dictum. We knew she respected our craft and unlike many designers we had worked with, Cipe read a manuscript fully before she would undertake a design project. It was also a time when writers and designers were teaming up together and discovering the value in creative collaboration. Lighting the way was Doyle Dane Bernbach, the award-winning young advertising agency that was putting writers and artists together in creative cells for the very first time.

Cipe and I would have the opportunity to work together again after many years. In 1966, I asked her to include Business Image to her client list. This was my creative company that I started in 1958 to help industry "connect" with the changing world of women. I had been retained by Condé Nast Publications to revitalize the image of several of its venerable magazines, among them *House and Garden*. Once more I had the opportunity to observe Cipe's unique ability to synthesize a creative problem and to skillfully produce a design solution. An example of this was when she composed an ingenious checkerboard of *House and Garden* colors to document the magazine's power to forecast and influence a color palette of choice for two decades. Most intriguing was the way Cipe demonstrated the harmonic relationship of each of the four-square blocks of color. Our collaboration was tested when Cipe would extract a headline from the manuscript I gave her, substituting it for the one I had proposed, explaining it would increase its visual power. In the same spirit, she would reorder paragraphs in a manuscript and tell me "it reads better and looks better!" I concurred. Years of mutual respect enriched and simplified discourse and debate.

H
&
G

House & Garden, best seller in the quality house field

20 twenty color-explosive years

A Condé Nast Publication

I never doubted Cipe's respect for the power of words and agreed with her efforts to insure readership in today's challenging multimedia visual age.

Cipe made design history in a historic time. In addition to her reputation for innovative design concepts, Cipe was in the vanguard of the Youthquake and Working Woman movements. She is credited with the emergence of two successful magazines, *Seventeen* and *Charm*. Together with their founding editor Helen Valentine, she embarked on a mission to serve and give visibility to its readers while alerting the nation to the importance of the teenage and working woman markets.

Cipe Pineles, art director
Above: *Seventeen*, October 1948.
Arnold Newman, photographer.
Right: *Seventeen*, July 1949.
Francesco Scavullo, photographer.
13¼ × 10½ in. each.
Courtesy of Hearst Communications.

***Charm*, January and March 1953**
Cipe Pineles, art director, William Helburn,
photographer. 11¼ × 8½ in. each.

CIPE PINELES TIMELINE

Excerpted, with permission from Martha Scotford, *Cipe Pineles: A Life in Design*. New York: W.W. Norton & Company, 1999.

1908	Born, Vienna, Austria, June 23, 1908
1920	Family home in Gliniany, Poland, invaded by Red Army; family moved to Vienna, Austria
1923	Family left Vienna and arrived in the U.S.A.
1926–1929	Studied at Pratt Institute, Brooklyn
1929–1930	Taught watercolor in Newark, N.J. Public School of Fine and Industrial Art
1930	Became a naturalized citizen on September 2
1930–1932	Took first design job at Contempora, Ltd., N.Y.C.
1932–1938	Worked as an assistant to Dr. M.F. Agha at Condé Nast on *Vogue* and *Vanity Fair* magazines
1935?	Met William Golden
1937	Worked in London on coronation issue of British *Vogue* magazine
1939–1946	Worked at *Glamour* magazine
1942	Became art director at *Glamour* magazine; Married William Golden on October 11, at City Hall, N.Y.C.; William Golden entered army in November
1945	Joined Golden in Paris as civilian advisor to *Overseas Woman*

1946	Returned to *Glamour* magazine, left Condé Nast for new job; William Golden returned from Europe in April
1947–1950	Cipe Pineles worked as art director of *Seventeen* magazine
1947?	Goldens bought house on Fire Island
1948	Pineles became the first woman member of the New York Art Directors Club
1950–1959	Worked as art director of *Charm* magazine
1950	Article published in *Studio News* on use of artists in *Seventeen;* Visiting critic at Parsons School of Design
1951	Tom Golden born March 30; adopted by Pineles and Golden
1953	Work reproduced in *Graphis* magazine
1955	Golden family moved in May to Stony Point, N.Y.; 9-page article on Cipe Pineles published in *Print* magazine
1959	Left *Charm* magazine, became art director of *Mademoiselle* William Golden died on October 23, 1959
1961	Left publication design to be an independent design consultant; Married Will Burtin on January 28, 1961
1961–1972	Worked for Will Burtin, Inc. as a design consultant
1962–1987	Taught Publication Design at Parsons School of Design
1964	Work included in AIGA's *American Magazine Show;* Worked on Illinois Pavilion with Burtin for New York World's Fair
1965–1970	Designer for Lincoln Center
1966–1969	Served on executive board of national AIGA
1968	Lincoln Center work included in *Graphis Annual*

1968	Russell Sage Foundation work in *Print Annual Report Best*
1970	Became Director of Publications for Parsons School of Design
1971	Included in *50 Prominent Alumni* at Pratt Institute of Art
1972	Will Burtin died on January 18, 1972
1975	Became the first woman elected to the ADC Hall of Fame
1976	Article published in *Art Direction* magazine
1977?	Accepted membership in Alliance Graphique Internationale
1978	Received Award for Excellence by Society of Publication Designers
1983	Parsons School of Design established Cipe Pineles scholarship
1984	Received Herb Lubalin Award from Society of Publication Designers
1985	Received Pratt Institute Alumni Achievement Award; Cover article published in *Print* magazine
1987	Retired from teaching at Parsons School of Design
1988	Work exhibited in *Women in Design*, Chicago show
1990	Work exhibited in *Graphic Design in America*, Walker Art Center
1991	Died at Suffern Hospital, Suffern, N.Y., January 3, 1991
1995	Article published in *Eye* magazine
1996	Named AIGA Medalist
1999	Monograph written by Martha Scotford, *Cipe Pineles: A Life of Design*, published by W.W. Norton & Company

Illustration from handwritten note,
July 14, 1971
Note from Cipe to Dorothy Gauntlett,
wife of Jack Gauntlett,
Director of Advertising, Upjohn.
Pen, 4¼ × 6⅜ in.
Courtesy of Dorothy Gauntlett,
Kalamazoo, Michigan.

The end of the note reads:
"London was so specially wonderful because…
we have many friends there and enjoyed lots
of social life. One night we heard someone
call after us: 'WILL, WILL, WILL BURTIN' &
it was Harry Tomlinson who said to his wife:
'Those two back views can be none other
than Will & Cipe.'"

COLOPHON

Design	Bruce Ian Meader and R. Roger Remington
Production	Marnie Soom and Amelia Hugill-Fontanel
Typefaces	Sabon designed by Jan Tschichold and Frutiger designed by Adrian Frutiger